Modern Sales

Leadership

Confidence, Process and Structure in Sales

Steve Knapp & Rob Taylor

Published by The Book Chief Publishing House 2021
(a trademark under Lydian Group Ltd)
Suite 2A, Blackthorn House, St Paul's Square, Birmingham, B3 1RL
www.thebookchief.com

Book Cover Design / Illustrations: Tracy Stead
Editor: Laura Billingham
Typesetting / Publishing: Sharon Brown
Proofreaders: Sharon Brown / Laura Billingham

THE BOOK CHIEF®

IGNITE YOUR WRITING

Table of Contents

Foreword

I am more than delighted to be providing this Foreword to Rob's first book and Steve's second 'Modern Sales Leadership' for several reasons.

First, I have known Steve for just a couple of years now, but I already know that he is 'the real deal'. He doesn't just talk about sales and sales leadership – he has been there, and very successfully too. He knows of what he speaks! This real-world experience is critical and it's a common theme amongst those who can truly deliver powerful advice and coaching.

Second, the title of the book says it all. The business world is changing and, in my opinion, will continue to change and evolve even more rapidly as we move forward. Of course, this then means that sales and especially sales leadership, is more needed than ever before. But Sales Leadership must really move with the times and adapt effectively, or risk being left behind.

And third? That's easy! I am lucky to have already read the book. There is something special about a short and concise book that somehow also manages to cram in so much advice. This book is packed with tips, knowledge, and wisdom. I own a copy of Steve's first book, 'Funnel Vision – Selling Made EASY' and that is exactly the same. If you don't own a copy, then buy it too.

Sales Leadership has always been challenging. It involves meeting difficult targets, herding sheep, motivation, discipline, real leadership by example and continuous serious effort in building the right culture and processes. Modern Sales Leadership touches on all these aspects. This is a book that is designed to be lifted up and read time after time. Got a problem? Get help here. Needing to change things? Learn the steps here. Developing the right processes? Open the book. As you read it, be ready to fold pages or use that marker pen!

Jim Irving, Author of The B2B Selling Guidebook, The B2B Leaders Guidebook and The B2B Sales Top Tips Guidebook.

Introduction

We are living in strange and changing times…

The pandemic and the repeated lockdowns it caused have given many of us the time to sit and reassess our place in the world - and what, if anything, we need to change to improve our own lives and the lives of those we work with.

The team at Plan.Grow.Do. have seen how people are acting differently in the workplace, the whole idea of turning up to the office 9 to 5 every day and devoting one's entire waking hours to work, has fallen by the wayside.

The millennial generation, those born between 1981 and 1996, are beginning to move into positions of authority. This age group will soon be calling the shots, and they have a very different way of looking at work, careers, job tenure and work-life balance.

Hybrid working, with a mix of home and office-based activity, has become the new norm for many people - including sales people - and this means that the whole concept of leadership has to evolve too. If you're a sales professional and are already a sales leader, or aspiring to be one, then you need to take a look at the way you (and your role) factor into this 'new way of doing things'.

When we came up with the concept for this short book (based to an extent on blogs and articles we had written over the past couple of years) it was to create a quick overview of selling and the art of selling, which would act as a kind of aide-memoire for the wonderful sales professionals we know are already out there trying to change the face of sales.

We look first at the history of selling and how and why the profession has had such a bad reputation, before moving on to look at how we can begin to move selling into the 21st century and beyond; into a new way of being and doing which sits more comfortably in this new post pandemic world.

This 'brave new world' is altering the way consumers buy - sales professionals like you need to adapt to the changing times. It's no longer enough to concentrate solely on targets - sell more, sell faster - modern consumers are knowledgeable, well researched, and they are not impressed by hard sell techniques. But who is out there helping sales managers and leaders through this transition? Well, the team at Plan.Grow.Do. for one!

Read on - and remember, only those of us who are already in the sales profession can take the next steps forward to effect the changes we want to see - that is to make selling into a career and a profession that millennials want to be a part of.

CHAPTER 1

A Brief History Lesson

Why is it that so many businesses shy away from using the words sales and selling?

And why do sales and the act of selling have such negative connotations for the general public?

Could it be because there is a certain reputation ascribed to salespeople, a certain stigma, that makes so many want to run a mile at the thought of actually being perceived as a salesperson?

Actually, YES, and it's such a shame. What's more, it needn't, and shouldn't, be this way, and as a sales leader in the 21st century, you are perfectly placed to change these outdated perceptions.

Let's take a quick history lesson to see if we can establish why sales has such a poor reputation.

Back to the Beginning
At the most basic level, selling involves one person exchanging goods or services for either money or other goods/services. Strictly speaking, the second scenario is 'bartering'; however, there is still the element of arriving at a suitable 'exchange rate' - which sounds like selling to us.

This means that for as long as humanity has been around, there has been some sort of selling going on. Yes, initially it would have been bartering as currency didn't exist until around 5,000 or so years ago, but for as long as people have needed things that others could supply, selling has existed.

How's that for a mind-blowing thought? There have ALWAYS been salespeople!

Here's another nugget which may surprise you: in approx. 1750 BC in what was then known as Mesopotamia, a King by the name of Hammurabi, had a code of law written which included a section designed to protect sellers: *Law #104: "If a merchant gives an agent grain, wool, oil, or any other goods to transport, the agent shall give a receipt for the amount, and compensate the merchant therefore, he shall obtain a receipt from the merchant for the money that he gives the merchant."*

Given that selling, in some form or another, has been around for most of human history, why then does there seem to be such a stigma about selling and salespeople these days?

Step up 'the Snake Oil' seller…
Back in the 1800s the US was busy building the First Continental Rail Road, and a lot of Chinese labourers were employed.

These labourers brought a product with them from home, which they used to reduce inflammation – it was made of oil from the Chinese Water snake. Allegedly they shared the oil with their American co-workers, who were suitably impressed and wished to replicate it. Unfortunately, Chinese Water snakes are not common in the US, and so 'alternatives' were used!

…and thus began the story of 'the Snake Oil' seller.

Travelling salespeople moving town to town selling their wares to a gullible market by claiming miraculous benefits and cures. Of course, by the time the oil was found to be of absolutely no use, the salespeople were long gone.

Who 'Invented' Modern Selling?
This honour falls to one John Henry Patterson, who was born in 1844 in Ohio and founded the National Cash Register Company (NCR) in 1884.

Mr Patterson was the first person (insofar as in known) to create a sales training manual, undertake direct mail and advertising, and provide his sales teams with a script which they were expected to follow to the letter. This manual was known as the 'NCR Primer', and any sales person who failed to demonstrate they had memorised the 450-word document was fired.

A little later, the 'Book of Arguments' was compiled – a compendium of how to overcome client objections.

Patterson was often quoted as saying that half of all lost sales could be attributed to the salesperson's failure to communicate. Definitely a man ahead of his time!

He also created the system of targets and bonuses, which, in one form or another, continues to this day. Salespeople were encouraged to sell more because that meant they earned more.

Greedy and unscrupulous individuals thus continued in the tradition of the 'Snake Oil' seller – selling things which people maybe didn't need, couldn't afford, or that weren't appropriate for them.

The Notorious Car Salesman!
How many people do you think have an image of a sharp-suited used car salesperson pop into their head when they hear the word 'salesman'?

We'd guess that it's probably quite a few, because so many people have had bad experiences buying a car, feeling pressured into buying, signing up for finance, added warranties etc.

Replace 'used cars' with any number of other products, and it's odds on you can think of occasions when an overly pushy salesperson has provided a horrible sales experience either for you or someone you know.

Those negative stereotypes stick in the brain and lead to the inevitable (if incorrect) belief that 'all salespeople are bad'.

Unfortunately, human nature being as it is, we do tend to dwell on the negative and thus, the idea that all salespeople are pushy, untrustworthy, 'out to con you' etc. is firmly engrained in the collective psyche!

Facing the Truth
As sales leaders, we have to face up to the unpalatable truth that sales and selling have an image problem. Much of this bad reputation may be based on past selling techniques, but there are still plenty of examples of poor sales approaches. For example, have you ever had that call offering you insurance for a washing machine you don't even have? Yep, that one when you've just sat down for the evening and you're kicking yourself because you answered the telephone.

Poor behaviour in the overall sales industry reflects badly on all of us, and it's way past time to address this situation and bring sales into the 21st-century post pandemic world.

Changing the Face of Sales

Consumers today, whether we're talking about individuals or businesses, are much savvier than in times past.

The internet has made experts out of everyone, and it's much easier to 'shop around' for both products and services. The repeated lockdowns only exacerbated this position, and sales needs to move and adapt accordingly.

According to research by media agency UM, a staggering 76% of UK buyers do online research before making a purchase; that may be referring to the individual consumer, but it would be a fair assumption that B2B purchasers also research intensively online. At least 47% of buyers look at between three and five pieces of content BEFORE choosing to engage with a salesperson, and 51% of buyers will rely on content to inform their buying decisions.

Sales teams need to be representatives and ambassadors of the company they work for, they must be conversant with the product(s) that's a given, BUT they must also be fully 'bought in' to the company's ethos and brand values (aka culture). The post pandemic world has changed, and sales processes need to have adapted to the new ways of conducting business. What worked 10, 7, 5, or even 3 years ago won't get you anywhere today.

Companies should adopt hiring plans which ensure that the right people are recruited to sales positions, ones who won't turn into 'Snake Oil' sellers!

Rewards packages that don't encourage making sales simply to achieve bonus levels can be designed, and continuous learning and development programs must be available. You, as a sales leader, have a huge role to play in ensuring recruitment and retention, and you must work with the management teams to create an environment where all the functions within an organisation interlock seamlessly.

Sales Behaviours
If sales, as a profession is going to move permanently away from the used car or snake oil salesman image, what needs to change, and how can you be a person of influence in bringing these changes about?

The 'in your face, pushy, overconfident approach' needs to go and be replaced with more measured behaviours. Remember that the customer has probably already done masses of research and could be simply looking for validation that they are making the right choice. A pushy salesperson could actually *lose* the sale, not *close* it.

Sales people should learn to listen as much, if not more, than talk. They should ask strategic questions and draw out information to work out exactly what the customer wants...not what the salesperson *thinks* they want.

The phrase 'he (or she!) could sell snow to an Eskimo' is often used in a derogatory way towards a salesperson. Let's turn this on its head...how can this ability be recognised as actually being a very valuable trait in a salesperson, instead of being seen as an underlining of a negative stereotype? How about highlighting the communication skills, empathy, and customer service aspects necessary to be such an innate salesperson? Take the emphasis away from the end result, closing the sale, to the process itself...the customer journey.

The customer journey refers to the customer's path, via touchpoints, to their decision to purchase. A customer doesn't usually decide to purchase an item immediately after finding out about it for the first time. We see the customer journey following these steps: Unaware, Aware, Consideration and Decision phases. Knowing this is how a buyer buys shouldn't it lead you to match your sales process to a similar set of touchpoints?

A seller can stack an opportunity greatly in their favour by appreciating this approach to sales, incorporating a blend of online and offline touchpoints. If it takes between 5 and 12 contact points to make a sale, how many of those can you make through your digital content that connects to how your buyer likes to buy?

You should be acting as an example for all the salespeople in your organisation, walk the talk, and practice what you are preaching. If you are seen as successfully adopting these 'softer' sales techniques, others will copy and follow your lead.

Ethics and Integrity in Selling
The millennial generation has a different way of thinking about business, who they work for and who they buy from. They are far more focused on values and ethics, both their own and the businesses they work for and deal with. They will resonate with those organisations that align with their own beliefs.

This generation (generally thought of as being born between 1981 and 1996) are now moving into positions of power, they are increasingly influencing company behaviours, and they are looking for ethical and integrity-based sales approaches. If you don't tick those boxes, if you can't earn their trust, then ultimately you will not make your sale.

A 2019 TrustRadius study found that Millennials are the largest B2B tech buyer group, making up 59% of B2B buyers, and 30% of them are lead buyers for their B2B brand. A recent report by Sacunas, a US-based B2B marketing agency, found that up to 73% of millennials are involved in product or service purchase decision-making at their companies.

And of that number, approximately one third said they were the main decision-maker when it came to buying.

That same report discovered that 80% of those surveyed agreed that a company's social and philanthropic efforts are a factor in their purchase decisions.

Aflac, a large American insurance provider, commissioned a 2018 survey of Corporate Social Responsibility (CSR), and a staggering 92% of the millennials questioned stated that they are more likely to purchase from an ethical company! This is obviously backed up by the stats mentioned above. Can you and your sales operation afford to miss out on this potential marketplace due to outdated sales practices?

Lead by example! It's time to start treating sales as a profession that people working in can be proud of and that the wider public view in favourable terms.

(Back to Snake Oil, in case you were wondering what was actually in the oil...in 1917, federal investors seized a shipment of 'Stanley's Snake Oil' and upon investigation discovered it contained mineral oil, a fatty oil believed to be beef fat, red pepper and turpentine...not a trace of anything snake related!)

Chapter 2

Sales Villains!

If someone's entire knowledge of the sales industry has been gained from watching TV programmes, it's hardly surprising that they may have a rather negative opinion of both sales and sales people.

Unfortunately, negative stereotypes abound and over time, they have become integrated into the communal psyche.

Sales and selling, as we mentioned in the previous chapter, have been around since the dawn of humanity. In fact, it could be said to be the second oldest profession (we'll leave it up to you to work out the oldest one…but suffice to say that includes 'selling' too!).

The how and why sales is portrayed so negatively is probably something worthy of a PhD thesis, but for now, let's just have a quick trawl through the stereotypes we are (still) being shown in TV and films that may influence the way salespeople are perceived. Recognising these negative character traits is a great way to begin to get rid of them!

We'll start with some UK based TV shows.

Arthur Daley - Minder
Charitably described as a lovable rogue, he was the epitome of a dodgy salesperson...'a Cockney wheeler dealer' in fact. Ostensibly a used car salesman, he also had a garage full of tat which he attempted to sell onto the unwary.

This quote from the show perfectly demonstrates the type of approach to sales that we are keen to see the back of: "*You make contact with your customer. Understand their needs. And then flog them something they could well do without.*"

To be fair to Arthur, he did at least get the first two statements correct!

'Del Boy' Trotter - Only Fools and Horses
A self-styled businessman, a market trader, running 'Trotters Independent Traders' from a suitcase or the back of his Robin Reliant car. He believed he could sell anything to anyone and had absolutely no qualms about how a sale was made (or even what he was selling), and he never saw himself as dishonest.

Albert Arkwright - Open All Hours
A miserly Northern shopkeeper with a penchant for ensuring no one left his shop without buying something - anything, even if they didn't want whatever it was they ended up purchasing.

Crafty, dishonest even, he may not be the archetypal slick salesman, but he ably demonstrates the 'Arthur Daley' school of selling…'flog em something they could well do without'!

Stateside Sales 'Villains'

'Wall Street', a 1987 movie, delved into the murky world of stocks and shares. Gordon Gekko (Michael Douglas) uttered the immortal line *'greed is good',* and the whole premise of the film is that anything goes in order to close a sale.

Taking the stockbroking theme even further, 'The Wolf of Wall Street' was a 2013 film chronicling the true story of Jordan Belfort, his career as a stockbroker and how his firm, Stratton Oakmont, engaged in rampant corruption and fraud.

Belfort practised 'hard selling' techniques which duped investors into parting with cash to buy stocks, thus inflating the value of said stocks. His company would then sell on the stocks they had previously purchased at low rates - earning $millions in the process.

'Glengarry Glen Ross' is a 1992 movie about the ruthlessness of hard sales. Four salesmen pitted against each other and vying to close sales, whilst motivated mainly by the fact that their jobs are on the line.

Nothing is ruled out in the desire to make a sale - morals are chucked out of the window in the quest to close.

What about 'Reality TV'?
One current TV show which really, really does no favours to the sales profession and those who work within it, is 'The Apprentice'. The contestants are seemingly encouraged to put ethics and personal morality behind them in order to 'win the prize', a philosophy that harks back to the worst sales techniques of the 1980s.

Common Themes
From the mundanity of a grocer's shop in the north of England to the glamour of Wall Street in the 1980s, there are key similarities in the portrayal of salespeople:

- They are predominately male
- They are liars (or at best deceptive)
- They are unscrupulous
- They are slick
- They don't care about their customers
- They are in it only for themselves

Shattering these Myths
Sales is chocked full of myths and stories about the way sales should be conducted...

In the second decade of the 21st-century, it's way past time that the sales industry moved from the practices of the past and caught up with the values and ethics of this era. It's down to sales leaders like YOU to make sure this happens.

Times have changed, and as millennials rise into positions of power within business, they will change even further; we salespeople need to keep up with these changes and adapt accordingly.

No longer will it suffice to rely simply on a never-ending churnover of sales staff with limited knowledge, training, or ability.

You and your sales teams need to reflect:
- Authenticity
- Trust
- Knowledge
- An ethical company culture

If sales is to permanently move away from the poor (and often deserved) reputation of the past, we all need to see there are better ways to sell – ways that work in the best interest of ALL parties to create a sales culture fit for the 21st Century.

Chapter 3

Sales Culture - Past, Present, and Future

While we're on the subject of 'sales culture' - how do you envision it changing as the world continues to adapt to a post-pandemic world with constantly evolving working conditions and the millennial generations increasing influence?

For the first time in our history we are living in a time when four generations can, and do, work in the same place at the same time; *baby boomers, gen x, millennials and gen z.* This undoubtedly brings with it not only challenges but more excitingly tremendous opportunity to align the experiences, expectation and values that each generation brings.

More and more we see buyers wanting to engage and build relationships with providers yet too often we see the same providers hiding behind the corporate message. A future culture should embrace the personality of the sales professional and provide the breathing space to allow them to show their values and how their values are supported by an organisation that reflects them and empowers that professional to be themselves.

We must stop hiding behind corporate banners and instead champion the brand and the business as it will align with us as people. People buy from people like themselves! We must not continue to hide what makes people, people.

We have some thoughts, which we'll share in a moment, but for now, it may be worth taking a quick overview at what sales culture used to be and what it's like right now…

The 'Old Style' Culture

In Chapter 2, we talked about 'sales villains' and the stereotypes the sector has been associated with for decades - if not centuries! The 'wide boys', the cheats, the over pushy persistent sellers…If sales and selling were associated with a culture in the past, it would have been a negative one, a very blokey, overtly masculine and supremely competitive (even combative) environment where 'selling the most' was infinitely more important than providing a customer with what they needed. The chief requirements for entering the profession were persistence, being in possession of a very thick skin and able to accept and absorb daily rejection. Before the online revolution, cold calling - either by phone or further back by knocking on doors - was a salesperson's main route to customers, and as many people loathe this kind of work, only a particular type of individual would enter the sector.

So the 'villains' persisted, influencing everyone's perception of sales being 'a not very nice arena in which to work'.

Present Day

Moving forwards in time and the profession began to develop; people like one half of Plan.Grow.Do. Steve Knapp, who could have found himself tarred with the same 'dodgy geezer' label as the likes of Arthur Daly, realised that a sale had to provide something of value to both parties. Steve began his sales career with a Saturday job on a fruit and veg stall in East London and ended up working for the multinational giant, Shell, for 30+ years…along the way increasing its market share in the mining sector of South Africa from 43% to 82% in just 2.5 years. It's fair to say, 'he knows a bit about selling', and he realised early in his career that the 'make a sale no matter how' methods of the past were no longer going to cut it in a changing world - it was time to take a look at literally rewriting the sales manual.

The way most salespeople operate today is very different from the old commission and target driven methodologies of not so very long ago. Yes, aggressive and pushy salespeople do still exist, but the buyers (both B2C and B2B) have moved on, with technology being the biggest driving force.

Thanks to the rapid and easy availability of information via the internet, 57% of purchase decisions are made *before* a buyer is in front of a salesperson (CEB's Marketing Leadership Council research), and they will not accept being sold to - the customer is in charge, not the salesperson.

Cold calling and prospecting, whilst not entirely dead, is very, very different when any prospect is already aware of the products and services on offer from any given company. Sales and marketing teams must work hand in hand to ensure that the information being put out is fit for purpose and tailored to suit the correct target audience. Learning to collaborate across departments has become an essential part of the new sales culture.

Sales personnel are themselves changing, in the 'good old days', it was not uncommon for people (in all sectors) to take a job on leaving school or university, and to stay with that employer until retirement age. Whilst perhaps less accurate in the sales sector, it was still more common for individual salespeople to stay with a company and 'climb the career ladder' (look at Mr Knapp, for example).

That is absolutely the exception today, with the average tenure in a role (across all age groups and sectors) being around 4 years, according to a U.S. study by the U.S. Bureau of Labor Statistics. This reduces to 2.8 years for the 'millennial' age group.

And, in the sales sector, the average tenure is even lower at 1.8 years (HubSpot). The average salesperson is still going to be driven by what they earn, but the younger employees, in particular, are asking for more than simply financial reward - they want to work with and for ethical companies that show high levels of integrity.

Millennials will make up 75% of the global workforce by 2025, according to Inc.com, and this generation, in particular, is very focused on the ethics and integrity of the companies they choose to work with. Research by Cone.com (U.S.) showed the following:

- 64% of Millennials consider a company's social and environmental commitments when deciding where to work
- 64% won't take a job if a company doesn't have strong corporate social responsibility (CSR) values
- 83% would be more loyal to a company that helps them contribute to social and environmental issues (vs 70% U.S. average)
- 88% say their job is more fulfilling when they are provided opportunities to make a positive impact on social and environmental issue

These stats apply equally to a salesperson as an office worker, and companies are beginning to wake up to this and adjust their overall culture to attract millennials.

Sales is already moving away from a macho, predominantly male environment, it's becoming more about how individuals can pull together as teams across an entire organisation, and its sales leaders who are helping to drive this culture change. More focus is being given to personalising the information given to prospects, and the faceless corporate output of the past is becoming less acceptable.

In a (very small) nutshell, the sales culture in the here and now is in a state of flux…

- Moving from hard-sell techniques to inform and educate the buyer using personalised touchpoints
- Moving from macho male to inclusivity
- Moving from purely 'sell more', 'earn more', to corporate social responsibility
- Moving from sales as a separate and stand-alone function to sales being fully integrated within an organisation
- Moving from long(er) tenure to job-hopping

Plan.Grow.Do. - the Future of Sales Culture
We've peered into our crystal ball to see how sales culture could change and develop still further; here's what we predict…

The trend towards companies and corporations working towards becoming ethically and integrity-driven will continue as more and more millennials demand a high level of corporate social responsibility (CSR) from the organisations they choose to work for. Organisations that fail to develop in such a way will struggle to recruit and retain any staff - including salespeople. Faceless corporates will be rejected by the consumer in favour of smaller, more local and regional based companies that can display a high level of CSR, and sales will need to adapt to fit into this new model.

Salespeople will increasingly be the ones selecting the organisations they want to work for, the job market will be an employee-driven one, and those companies offering what the prospective employee seeks will win out over those offering 'the same old, same old' employee packages. Salespeople will expect remuneration that reflects their sales success but will also look for opportunities to contribute to the greater good - Google, for example, allows paid time out for volunteering. Salaries will be less about commission and bonuses and more about great pay for great work and opportunities to grow and develop.

Salespeople will become sector specialists, not company experts; they will expect to move between different organisations in the same sector easily, and often in order to progress their own career.

At the same time, buyers will continue to become ever more knowledgeable and will expect a salesperson to know more than they do; blustering through a sales presentation won't cut it

Diversity, Equality, Inclusion

One issue we need to address - the 'elephant in the room' if you like - is the lack of diversity in sales at the moment. It was blokey, all guys together, lots of drinking, deals on the golf course etc., with family unfriendly hours. Recently though, sales has opened up to become more inclusive.

And by inclusive, we mean people of all gender identities, race, colour, and physical ability should now be considering sales as a career.

This should become the norm, as more and more of the traditional 'legwork' of securing leads moves online, there is no longer any need to physically travel to a buyers location, unless, or until that lead translates into a genuine prospect. This opens the doors for many more people to give sales a go - and that is what we hope to see happening.

Millennials and Generation Z (often referred to as Digital Natives or the iGeneration, the cohort that comes after the Millennials born somewhere between 1996 and 2012) think differently, they behave differently, and they interact with each other and with the world in a different way to us older sales professionals. We could learn as much from them as we could teach - if we opened our eyes and ears.

We can also see the barriers between individuals and organisations breaking down; there will be nowhere for corporates to hide as people seek out (and find) information on the internet, be that good or bad.

A fully transparent online presence will be vital for all organisations and will have to address the ways millennials and Generation Z consume media and information.

Short videos (30 secs) and personalised content will be king, these buyers will be buying from a person, not a company, and sales teams will need to become completely customer-centric, not relying on the same content for each prospective customer.

In short, we see the sales culture of the future being a story of collaboration; collaboration internally between all teams and departments; collaboration in how information is shared; collaboration between individuals as they move in and out of companies but remain in the same sector; and finally, and most importantly - between sellers and buyers.

Here are the key points:

- Faceless corporations won't cut it anymore with the consumer
- Ethically led organisations will prosper
- Salespeople will become sector specialists, not company experts
- Personalisation - people to people selling will be key
- Buyers will become experts, so there will be nowhere to hide for the salesperson
- Collaboration will be critical

Chapter 4

Why a Strong Sales Culture is Essential

Whether you are a recently appointed sales leader or a seasoned veteran, you will have heard the term 'sales culture' being bandied about; we've even talked about it in the previous chapter. Do you know what 'sales culture' is though, what it means and how getting it right can have a massive impact on your sales results?

Does the term make you cringe?

Perhaps it sounds like one of those high level 'management speak' phrases that can't possibly be applied to you?

Creating a winning sales culture in a virtual world is hard, and transforming an underperforming sales team into a well-oiled sales machine doesn't happen by luck. Yet many companies try to grow sales by simply putting more pressure on the sales team, reminding them of their increasing quotas and highlighting how much they're behind the plan.

Companies invest a lot of time and money into better products or more marketing, which doesn't hurt, but only further masks the true underlying gap. The reality is the team are underperforming because the true gap is that there isn't a winning sales culture.

"CULTURE EATS STRATEGY FOR BREAKFAST"

PETER DRUCKER

It doesn't matter if an organisation is a multinational operation or an SME, if sales and the sales force are not seen as an essential, and more importantly, an integral part, then the business will not reach its full potential.

At the most basic level, if staff do not feel that they are all working towards a common goal – namely increasing income (aka sales) – then there will always be discord and inter-departmental rivalry.

For example, sales are doing really well, and they are all exceeding their targets.

But the accounts team are not keeping up with the increased need to invoice/credit check/credit control and therefore the money is not landing in the company bank accounts in a timely fashion.

The result is that the sales team are disillusioned because they can't see the rewards for their successes as quickly as they should.

In another scenario, the sales team are again performing well, but production is slow to scale up to reach demand.

Or how about the purchasing team have not been informed of the latest sales drive and therefore have not placed the necessary supply orders that will be required to increase production.

And so it goes on.

The crux of it is that every person within an organisation needs to be putting sales at the top of their agenda – regardless of whether they are part of the sales team itself.

It's only by doing that, by creating cohesion between all the teams in an organisation, that sales can be maximised, and this type of cohesion needs a charismatic leader to pull everyone together.

In a nutshell then, sales culture may be described as "putting sales at the heart of every business process".

That may be a little simplistic, but you get the gist!

What's the Sales Culture in your current organisation?

Stand back for a moment and take a good long look...
Be objective, try to see things as if you were an outsider looking in. Consider it a full 360° review of the existing operations.

What are the current sales figures, and are they consistent month on month, or do they fluctuate?

Are there any external reasons for fluctuations, for example seasonality, or are the differences solely attributable to the success (or otherwise) of the sales team?

How do the various teams or departments interact? Is there rivalry (or worse) between different teams?

Are the accounts team seen as 'blockers' by the sales force or the sales team seen as being 'pushy' or 'arrogant' by the rest of the company?

Examining the current situation should help to determine not only what sort of sales culture currently exists, but also what the overall company culture is. You may be surprised at some of the things you discover!

There is a school of thought that businesses should be driven from the bottom upwards, but whilst engaging everyone within a company is absolutely vital, at the end of the day, the reality is it's the leadership team that really shapes culture and ethos.

You are a sales leader and thus perfectly positioned to make an impact on the overall culture within a business.

In other words, you need to drive culture change from the top down.

> ## "TRAIN PEOPLE WELL ENOUGH SO THEY CAN LEAVE, TREAT THEM WELL ENOUGH SO THEY DON'T WANT TO"
> RICHARD BRANSON

This sort of approach is one that all businesses should look at adopting – it demonstrates a corporate culture that places employees as the key assets. You can link this approach directly to creating a positive and enabling sales culture.

Every person within the organisation (be that 2 or 222 of them) has to understand and embrace the fact that without sales, there is no business.

Put that in an entirely person-centred sentence – "Without sales, you will have no job".

Such a bold statement of reality tends to have a way of focusing people's attention!

Everyone, from the most junior staff member right up to the board, needs to understand the importance of sales, how the sales process works (*see chapter 9*) and what their role is in ensuring consistently high sales levels.

There is absolutely no point in giving sales teams targets if they have no support from the rest of the business. Equally, there is no point rewarding sales teams for hitting their targets whilst not also rewarding the support teams, because just as a car won't work without fuel, neither can sales people operate in isolation.

Nothing in isolation

Isolating salespeople, treating them differently, setting them apart from everyone else, simply serves to alienate them from the rest of your workforce.

When creating sales strategies (*see chapter* 8), targets etc., ensure that the other departments are included in the process – or, at the very least, kept informed.

Aligning business operations towards sales has been shown to result in a higher probability of sales closures. According to a 2014 study by *Math Marketing*, organisations that are aligned have a 67% higher probability that marketing-generated leads will close. Yet research by *Bizible* shows that over 30% of marketers feel that they are not aligned with their sales team.

Translating these stats into bottom-line results shows that tightly aligned sales and marketing operations achieved 24% faster three-year revenue growth and 27% faster three-year profit growth. (Sirius Decisions).

Information is powerful if it contributes to collaboration

Information is key to a company's success, but all too often, you find departmental managers holding onto things because they feel it gives them an edge over a colleague.

Competition can be a useful tool, particularly within a sales environment, but it can be at the expense of collaboration.

Rather than separate pockets of information residing at departmental level, work towards companywide "all hands" meetings where everyone can have their say and you can share strategy. If your organisation is too large to do this, have representation from each level (and ensure the most junior are included). You will need to get the backing of senior managers in order to make this work, but hopefully, they will understand the benefits and come onboard.

Try something new

A fresh perspective can be extremely useful, and younger staff are often able to see things in a totally different way.

Try making these meetings standing ones – it tends to keep them brief, and it also negates the hierarchy situation that happens when seated around a table.

Instead of imposing ideas, ask for input.

Is there something the accounts team do that drives your sales team mad?

Does the marketing team make promises that neither sales nor production can fulfil?

Are your sales teams making promises to customers that just can't be kept so, in turn, putting pressure on other departments?

Perhaps a junior employee has spotted something that can be improved, a system that may have been in place for ages, but they spot a way to make it better?

Look at the existing staff roster, the terms and conditions and remuneration but also look at how you can improve them – don't assume that 'good rates of pay' are the be-all and end-all.

Today's workforce (particularly millennials) often have a different approach to their working life.

Work-life balance is not something you hear much of in a sales environment, but it should be factored into your recruitment strategy.

If your staff turnover is high, find out why and fix it.

Perhaps people have been driven away by unrealistic expectations that result in burnout?

Maybe your packages are not reflective of others in your industry?

Are managers the problem?
Your aim is to create the kind of workplace that people want to come to and want to stay with.

Create a place where your people feel valued, listened to, and really believe that their contribution matters – whatever their role is.

Creating the right sales culture for the organisation may mean that you do have to consider letting people go...not an easy decision. However, as you undertake a companywide review and begin to implement new collaborative practices, it will very quickly become apparent if there are any sticking points (or rather resistant people).

To be honest, such individuals may begin to feel so out of place in a revised culture (particularly if they had been 'getting away' with behaviours that are contra to your new culture) that they may decide to move on without prompting.

You will by now have realised that creating the kind of sales culture that will not only drive sales teams to excellence but will also motivate the entire workforce is going to be neither easy NOR quick. It will however be worth it.

"They need to have sold to understand the process, but being good at sales doesn't make a good sales manager" Director in the Recruitment industry (source: LinkedIn poll 2021)

Chapter 5

Sales Culture and Building Sales Behaviour

A good team…but something is missing?

> **"EFFECTIVE LEADERSHIP IS DOING THE RIGHT THINGS.
> EFFECTIVE MANAGEMENT IS DOING THINGS RIGHT".**
> STEPHEN COVEY – 7 HABITS OF HIGHLY EFFECTIVE PEOPLE

You may find you are achieving results, and the short term is looking great. You may feel your effective leadership and coaching is building a fantastic culture, but there may also be a risk that the sustainability of these results is unknown.

Let's explore what could help define and create an effective sales culture across the team.

The sales team is likely to be increasing in size
In a recent report produced by the East Midlands Chamber; *"Skills Recovery in South Yorkshire",* it was believed that 45% of businesses in manufacturing expect to see an increase in their workforce, with *24% of businesses saying they will find it difficult to recruit in sales, 24% finding it difficult to recruit for business development, 23% senior managers and 20% in finding the right leaders.*

51

What primary skill are people looking for in their B2B sales recruit?

In a quick online poll researching the primary skills that those recruiting B2B sales professionals will be looking for, *tenacity* was cited as a key attribute that interests the recruiters or leaders, with *resilience* a close second. Nobody cited *compliance* as the primary factor in their B2B recruitment search.

Tenacity

Tenacity is that fierce blend of *determination, persistence, and grit*. It's interesting that we want people to be tenacious in their work. It suggests that we are looking for people who can think on their feet, use their initiative, and be prepared to proactively seek opportunities. But perhaps recruiting Mr or Ms Tenacious without the development of structure or process could lead to them becoming a bit of a loose cannon or a person who develops habits not consistent with the culture you're trying to create.

Resilience

Resilience traits tend to include *empathy, calmness under stress, hope, and self-control.* It's fair to say in sales that there may well be some knockbacks. *No* might be a word to become friendly with, and the ability to handle objections, accept rejection and understand when the opportunity is not a good one, is a good skill to have.

However, if the confidence and up-skilling required for our resilient team to perform is not created, resilience will be tested over time. A person may become disconnected, more hesitant to try new things, and become more withdrawn from the team.

An effective sales culture is what to aim for.

Three common themes are evident when it comes to strategically building and improving sales teams; *Confidence, process, structure* – three powerful components that help more prominently at different stages and in different parts of the business but each as equally important as the other in support of your sales team or new sales recruits.

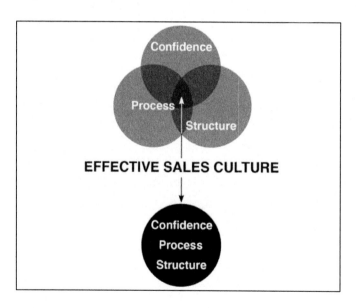

As a sales leader, you may believe that your business has *elements* of the three key aspects of an effective sales culture (and you may be correct in your belief), but without a balance of each, you may have a tendency to focus on developing the element with which you are most aligned personally, whilst offering feedback and bias based on the lens through which you view the wider sales function.

This can lead to an unbalanced view of your wider sales team and challenges the ability to sustain the winning sales success you might enjoy in the short term. Despite recruiting or focusing on the primary skillset you set out to enhance, you may see an increase in staff churn, internal challenges and a disconnected team. Let's look a little more at the challenges these components bring and the opportunities which can be presented by improving confidence, process, and structure to help our tenacious and resilient new recruits.

Support your sales team with the components of an effective sales culture.

How to create a culture to support the tenacious sales professional.
Let's unpack this a little more and see how the components of an effective sales culture can benefit a sales team's skills.

Let's take Mr Tenacious as a first example. Mr Tenacious is determined, persistent and has grit and desire. We could assume that Mr Tenacious is quite a confident addition to the team, which on the face of things, is fantastic. But if we bring Mr T into the business with no process, we run the risk of not giving them a steer or direction on what is expected. If Mr T comes into a team that *'doesn't do it that way'*, without the framework that process can deliver, you might soon find a fractured team behaving in different ways to what should be expected.

Risk of lacking processes include:

- Lack of accountability
- Poor service
- Knowledge gaps
- Rudderless

If confidence is a missing component of your sales culture as recognised by the risks above, you can expect several benefits by working to remedy this exclusion, but perhaps recognising this gap is the biggest first step.

Expected benefits of improving the confidence of the sales team:

- Agile to customer needs
- Loyal and more open to and embracing of change

- Self-accountable
- Happy to take responsibility
- increased overall effectiveness.

"let sales people sell and managers manage - I really do not understand why so many organizations still take their best sales people and make them managers - guess what - they stop selling and start becoming administrators" Sales Consultant (source: LinkedIn poll 2021)

So, where does structure fit?

The component parts of a sales culture that could better support the skillset that our tenacious and resilient sales team bring to the sales function has already been addressed. However, at all levels and roles, we can encompass *structure* as the third component of our sales culture. As an organisation, you may focus on process to help *Mr Tenacious,* and you may have built a confidence-building environment to support the resilience of the new team. But without tapping into an effective structure, you may be open to more risks that can manifest in several ways. *Do you recognise any of these traits within your organisation?*

The risk of not addressing lack of structure:

- Middle management without direction
- Disconnected team and management
- Ideas but no consistent approach

- Difficult to measure success or failure or 'good ideas'

Expected benefits for improving your sales structure:

- Faster decision making
- Improved operating efficiency
- Greater employee performance
- Reduced conflict
- Better communication
- Repeatable and accountable at all levels

Here's a 1 to 10 list of how to start to build a winning culture in your sales teams:

1) Follow your salespeople

The first thing a sales coach or trainer will do when taking on work for a client is - nothing! Actually, that isn't quite true, they will listen and watch the Sales Professionals and Sales processes in operation. They do this because when it comes to why they aren't producing, salespeople can rarely tell you, but they can show you.

2) Monitor daily activity

A mechanic wouldn't look at your car and just tell you what was wrong with it; he'd check the engine and the electrics or hook it up to a machine to get readings. You have to do the same thing for your sales team.

Set Sales Expectations, these would be six to eight daily revenue-producing activities that every Sales Professional is measured against. Whatever you choose is fine, but the data is essential for monitoring because numbers never lie.

3) Drive activity more than results
Sales is, and always will be, a numbers game. Whoever sees the most qualified number of prospects in the shortest time has the best chance of winning. Salespeople have little control over who buys and who doesn't so spend more time pushing them to increase activity, and results will increase as a by-product.

4) Lose the bad apples
Experience shows that the average sales manager knows immediately whether or not a person is going to make it, yet it typically takes six to nine months to let that person go. Bad attitudes, low work ethic and people who undermine leadership are a virus to your sales team. The longer you let them stay around, the more it is costing your company and the more they are infecting those around them.

5) Learn to Recognise Success
Start recognising your top leaders and sales professionals more publicly. One of the fastest ways to get results is by creating an incentive plan for driving activity.

You can come up with fun, affordable incentives that create an immediate spike in activity. Top producing sales professionals are a different breed, and it's amazing how far they'll go to get a £50 iTunes card or get their name called in a team meeting.

6). Create a purpose
Selling is emotional. Selling takes energy. And many salespeople need to be sold on the greater good of what they're doing. They need to understand that they are contributing to the bigger picture. You can even have them come up with their own purpose by just capturing their responses in a group setting to the questions, "What do we believe in and why are we here?" Salespeople need vision, and it's the job of leadership to help that vision come alive.

7). Elevate the sales professional
Sales professionals are amazing. They are often among the highest income earners in a company, and they should be. They battle doubt and rejection every single day. In your talk and actions, ensure that the importance of the sales function to the other departments in the company is highlighted.

8). Invest in sales training! (but make sure it's the right kind!)
It's a company's job to give its sales professionals the tools and training they need to succeed in their position.

Sales cultures have well-defined systems to help their salespeople grow, learn, and achieve. This is especially important for new hires, but you also need to have some way to deliver ongoing advanced sales training ideas for your entire sales team.

If you don't think this is important, then determine how much it costs you on average to hire someone and multiply that by the number of salespeople who didn't make it last year; you'll quickly see it's worth the investment.

9). Create more accountability

Most good sales professionals crave and welcome regular accountability. Spending regular one-on-one time with your people not only gives you a chance to mentor and train with them; it shows that what they do is important and that you care about their success. It also means you can create a bit of healthy tension as you push for results.

10). Create sales scripts

Most salespeople are far less technically proficient at selling than they think. They are reticent to call on new business because they aren't good at it, and they don't know what to say. While they will complain about being forced to say word-for-word scripts, you must have them available, and they must work.

A sales team without sales scripts is like a business without a business plan; it lacks focus and is inconsistent. Note, we are not talking about a robotic approach to sales but a planned and prepared one that helps the seller guide and control the sales meeting.

Chapter 6

Attributes of a Winning Sales Coach

One way to develop a successful sales team is to work with a sales coach, and as a sales leader yourself, you may also take on a coaching role, but have you ever considered what the attributes of a winning sales coach are?

What are the qualities that make a top sales coach, manager, and leader?

Results, retention, recruitment – The 3 R's

Trying to categorise the top qualities of a coach and sales leader is no easy task.

Top coaches will come from different backgrounds and have different styles, but they know how to connect with people, inspire quality performance and get results. Sport is always a good reference point for top coaches.

The key qualities you'll see in a great sales coach and sales leader are:

- Leadership
- Knowledge
- Knowing Your Team
- Motivation
- Consistency and Effective Communication Skills.

Let's take a quick walkthrough and explain why each is important and offer you a few points to consider to help raise your game.

Leadership

A great coach should be an exceptional leader with the ability to unify a group and make them committed to a single purpose. (see chapter 7 for more about leadership versus management skills).

The goal of great coaching is to guide, inspire and empower an individual or a team to achieve their full potential. You should ensure you are:

- Accessible and available. When people want to see you and talk to you, prioritise that time over " other stuff".
- Creating the direction, empowering, allowing the space to operate and guiding the outcomes. Not micromanaging.

Your job is to create heroes - not be one.

"They should be good at coaching as well as good at selling. They need both. Pulling in a great non-selling manager would mean they would only be great at part of the job. Reps couldn't rely on that non-selling manager to help them strategize on deals or help them close deals" Sales Coach (source: LinkedIn poll 2021).

Knowledge
A great coach should have an in-depth understanding of the skills they are coaching. This does not necessarily have to come from personal experience, but a sales coach needs to have an understanding of the fundamental skills to advanced tactics and strategies involved in sales.

- Tune into podcasts and read. There is so much out there to assist your journey to becoming a sales leader and coach
- Find a mentor or coach for yourself. Many will have walked in your shoes, and could help you avoid making unnecessary mistakes

Motivation

Coaches need to be able to convey passion to their team members and to inspire them to get the most out of their performance.

A successful coach will possess a positive attitude and enthusiasm for the business and the sales goals. This, in turn, inspires their team to excel.

Motivation might also involve keeping the coaching sessions engaging and challenging. Exploring the "art of the possible" can be very motivating.

- Working on your mindset by creating a well-being routine will keep you at the top of your game
- Make targets realistic. Not too big, not too small, but with enough stretch to keep motivation high
- Take the time in every team meeting or team call to celebrate successes

Know Your Team

The key to successful coaching is being aware of the individual differences of your team members. Some coaching tactics work better on different personality types, so it is important to tailor communication and motivation based on specific personalities.

To achieve this, a coach needs to pay attention to the emotions, strengths, and weaknesses of each person in the team. Knowing the individual also involves having empathy for the person.

Coaches need to care deeply about their people, and a coach needs to be willing to be a mentor and counsellor, as well as a coach.

- Spend time with each team member. Don't just focus on the star or bottom performers
- Commit to a 30-minute meeting every week with each of your team members. This will build trust and create transparency
- Don't focus solely on performance in your weekly meetings, as personal circumstances will often impact performance

Consistency

If a coach wants to change an attitude, alter the plan, or improve skills, the coach needs to be consistent in the message they are delivering. Salespeople will learn by hearing the same message constantly and consistently.

Constantly moving the goal posts and forever changing priorities will confuse and demotivate a sales team.

Don't give them the "wriggle room" to avoid and dodge accountability, as they will use the changes as reasons and excuses.

- Keep consistency in purpose, goals and objectives. Know which way is north and use team meetings, team calls and internal communication to constantly reinforce the message
- Trust the process. Having a common sales process or methodology will create commonality in language and application
- Reduce KPIs. Too many targets will confuse people. Find the key metrics and stick with them

Effective communication skills
Needless to say, a great coach will possess exceptional communication skills.

An effective coach is able to set defined goals, express these goals and ideas clearly to their team, give direct feedback, reinforce key messages, and acknowledge success.

Listening is also a part of effective communication, so a coach should be a compassionate listener who welcomes comments, questions, and feedback.

- Don't be the loudest voice. Set the scene and encourage others to contribute. The quiet voices may be the deeper thinkers and have the best way forward
- Always ask questions and never assume you know it all. You might have an extra stripe on

your arm or one more pip on your lapel, but don't look to be seen as the "font of all knowledge"

- Prepare for meetings. Selling can be emotional. Hitting or missing targets brings all sorts of challenges and reactions. By preparing, you'll be factual, logical, fair, and transparent

"I think they need to understand how to listen and match solutions" Director (source: LinkedIn poll 2021)

Chapter 7

Why Successful Leadership Matters

The last chapter focused on why sales coaching should be a vital part of developing your sales teams, now let's take a look at how your strong leadership is vital in order to not only implement a strategy to improve sales culture but to ensure it is consistently maintained.

The Difference Between Managing and Leading
You may think that there is no difference between managing and leading a team or an organisation, but there really is. Look at the following infographic:

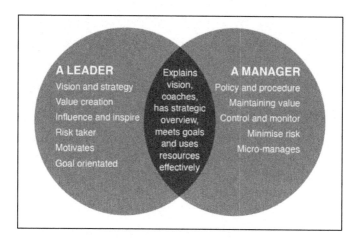

Can you see the differences?

A leader tends to be charismatic and attract people who will follow them; leaders not only talk the talk but walk the walk, which inspires their followers. They are often creative problem solvers and will take risks to achieve goals.

A manager may have many similar surface-level characteristics to a leader but dig a little deeper, and you tend to find that they are more rule and protocol-driven than a natural leader. They will still get results, but they rarely inspire the staff they supervise in quite the same way.

Some people have the rare ability to combine both the rigid strictures of management with the transformational and inspirational qualities of leadership (see the intersecting segment on the infographic) – if you are one of those people, bravo! You have a head start on becoming an amazing sales leader.

"I see leaders being like a pacer in a marathon. It's the sales reps victory but it's the pacers service that champion them to victory" VP of Sales (source: LinkedIn poll 2021)

How is your Sales Force Structured?
Whether you have one sales team or multiple, the way they are organised, the sales culture within the organisation and the *leadership* from the top is going to affect their success.

Do you have a sales manager (or managers)? If so, look at the way he/she operates. Are they rule-driven micro-managers who leave your teams feeling uninspired and lacking in motivation? Are they purely target driven, forever hammering home the 'more sales' message whilst constantly upping their team's sales targets?

Look at staff turnover within your sales force. Is it high? If you have multiple sales teams, is there a pattern of higher turnover in any of the teams in particular? If there is, could the manager of that team be the problem?

Build Successful Teams

There may need to be a root and branch examination of the organisation, and things may need changing around to achieve a successful company structure (refer back to Chapter 3 for a wider explanation of creating a new company culture). Hopefully, as the sales leader, you will be able to impress the importance of such a comprehensive re-evaluation on the rest of the leadership team.

All the management areas need to be linked - finance cannot stand apart from marketing and the sales force cannot work in isolation.

Instigate training sessions, starting with your sales managers (if you have them).

Coach them in how to motivate their respective teams by understanding that there is no one size fits all methodology. Show them how to work with their teams as groups of individuals who all require coaching in subtly different ways.

Hire salespeople who fit within the company and sales cultures and ensure they understand the sales expectations from the get-go. Make goals/targets high but achievable and incentivise your teams appropriately.

A company needs strong leadership that everyone looks to for inspiration, motivation, and guidance. The heads of departments need to have leadership as well as management skills, and everyone needs to work together.

Salespeople, particularly those who are managing teams, tend to be target driven, but individuals within a team may not be so driven. You, as the sales leader, need to understand what makes an individual tick, what incentives/bonuses work best.

Are they team players who like to compete against other team members, or do they prefer to compete only against their own past results?

Mentoring as well as selling abilities should be encouraged amongst sales teams, and teams should support and learn from each other, acting as a cohesive entity as opposed to a bunch of people constantly competing against each other to be the best.

This is not to say that competition is bad…of course it isn't! In fact, salespeople are naturally competitive and want to meet or exceed their targets, but you need to find a way that encourages competition whilst fostering collaboration.

Having the right people heading up sales teams is vital. That is not to say that a sales manager must also be a sales leader - that is, after all, your role!

Look back to the infographic at the beginning of this chapter - a leader is ultimately a visionary and strategist, able to see the bigger picture and inspire others to achieve their best in order to attain goals and targets. Whereas a manager is more concerned with the day to day processes and documentation of results.

Sales Leader
What qualities are important for you to successfully operate in this role?

A sales leader should operate at a strategic level, creating and maintaining a positive sales culture throughout the organisation.

Creating and communicating the vision and direction and keeping a 360° overview of the entire business.

A leader needs to be able to pull everyone in the organisation together, working towards the same goals, targets, and aspirations – whatever role or level they are.

"Sales Management and Sales are two very different skill sets. You see it all the time… reps get promoted and make terrible managers. Not always. But sometimes" Director of Sales (source: LinkedIn poll 2021)

Sales Manager(s)
If you happen to have a sales manager who also has leadership skills, then well done, hold onto them at all costs and help them develop to support you!

If not, nurture their process-driven side and ensure they have the necessary tools at their disposal in order for them to track and measure sales and targets. Encourage them to create and replicate successful processes and share their systems with other teams.

The most successful sales managers are target and deadline-driven. They stand and fall by the sales figures they and their team(s) achieve.

In a 2015 interview of over 1000 sales leaders for the Harvard Business School, 75% of well-performing sales managers reported holding their teams to a high degree of accountability by consistently measuring results against targets.

This level of accountability can however, sometimes mean a lack of empathy and understanding of how to help underachieving sales staff. Ensure therefore that your managers receive the training to help them support their team(s) in ways other than mere insistence that targets are met!

"The best sales people don't necessarily make the best sales managers as they two jobs require different skillsets, but a sales manager needs to understand and appreciate what their teams are going through and you can't get all you need from a textbook" Business Solutions Specialist (source: LinkedIn poll 2021).

A Cohesive Organisation

A successful business needs to have the right culture - top to bottom, bottom to top. No matter how large the organisation, every employee needs to know they matter, that their contribution counts.

Individual departments need to ensure that they are integrated into the whole – no one department can function without another, and the business cannot operate optimally unless all the disparate parts work together.

In a nutshell, your role as a sales leader should encompass…

- Finding and retaining the best staff
- Looking for managers with true leadership potential
- Ensuring staff are compensated appropriately
- Ensuring everyone is aware of the company vision, values and ethos
- Ensuring sales is at the heart of all business processes
- Ensuring departments collaborate rather than compete against each other
- Knowing the customers and making sure you 'sell' to them appropriately

Sell BETTER not just MORE!

Chapter 8

Why Every Business Needs a Sales Strategy

In this chapter, we are taking a look at sales strategies - what they are and why you need them; after all, even the most inspirational of leaders need a framework on which to build success.

Basic Definition of Sales Strategy
Here's a clue – it isn't simply throwing stuff out there (including the sales team) and just hoping something will 'stick' and result in a sale.

NO!

A sales strategy is a detailed plan which establishes the direction to take and how to go about developing sales processes (see Chapter 9) in order to ensure consistent sales and therefore income.

Starting Over!
When they first started out, new businesses would have been glad of any sales, no matter where (or how) they happened. The problem is that if an organisation remains stuck in this kind of mindset, then it is unlikely to have created a fully cohesive sales strategy.

You, as a sales leader, need to be able to take control and ensure that the organisation is able to grow, develop and strategise, in other words…Plan.Grow.do.

This section is entitled 'Starting Over' for a reason, it's time to take a really good look at where you are now, what is working in terms of bringing in sales and what needs to be completely revisited, revamped and redone.

It can be very easy for people to get stuck in the 'we've always done it this way', or 'this has always worked before' mode of thinking, you need to be able to develop the people within the sales function to a 21st century way of doing things.

Getting Back to Basics
What About the Customers? Does the organisation know where they are currently coming from? If not, why not?

- What does the ideal customer avatar look like - is there actually more than one?
- What do customers say on social media about the organisation? Can they leave reviews?
- Is there an unexplored market to consider?

Look at the Product. Now this may sound so basic that you will wonder why it merits a mention, but what are you selling? Is it a physical product(s) or a service?

Take a good look at whatever it is - analyse it. What will buying it give customers?

- Does it solve a problem(s)?
- Does it tackle a pain point?
- Or is it a luxury item - something that people desire but don't really need?
- Are you selling direct to consumers, or is your market B2B?

Get these points straight in your head because they will affect your selling strategy.

What is the Current Marketing?

- Look at current marketing tools and bring the marketing team in on this
- What does the social media presence look like? Has the message changed since the early days?
- Is there actually an over-reliance on social media? Has the organisation become a little complacent, even seduced by online channels?
- Are the marketing messages conveying everything they need to?

- Should different social media platforms be considered?
- What is the following like on the platforms currently being used? Does one outperform another? If so, why?
- Are mailshots (both physical and email) used, and if so, who do they target?
- How do you measure the results of your marketing activity?

What you are doing here is stripping back everything – establishing what has worked so far and what needs changing going forwards.

Starting to Plan

Right - you've looked at the current situation. You understand what is working with the existing marketing, and you have a grip on your target audiences.

Now you can start to strategise.

Work to establish realistic sales targets based on the organisation's financial needs and capabilities - create a Sales Forecast.

Sales Forecast. Don't pull figures out of the air; make sure targets are achievable.

- Base forecasts on past performances
- Look at existing customers – what are their buying habits, and can they be influenced to buy more or a different product?

- Break down the forecast into monthly/weekly figures and by customer and product. How many leads and conversions will be required to hit the targets?
- How many salespeople will be required to reach these targets - is it more or less than you currently have?
- What sort of activity is needed to meet the targets; can you quantify this in cost terms?

Targeting and Reaching Customers (Sales Channels) Get your marketing and salespeople in the same room!

Based on the sales forecast you have created, plan out how your marketing and advertising can target the customer base you wish to focus on (this may vary seasonally or even month to month, so take this into account).

- Does new marketing material need to be created? Get the input of the people on the ground; they are closer to the customer and will have a good idea of what does (and doesn't work)
- Segment your audience in order to run highly targeted campaigns
- Can existing customers be upsold to?
- Can existing customers be persuaded to give recommendations (a referral scheme)?

- Work on customer retention ideas - it is easier to keep a customer than seek a new one
- Do you need to revise social media campaigns (and platforms) to target key audiences?
- Do you even need to consider re-branding?

Sales and marketing need to work together; they are each one side of the same coin after all. It is pointless having super-duper marketing materials if the sales team don't know about them; imagine being a salesperson dealing with a customer who points out something in a leaflet or online campaign that they were completely unaware of. Not only does that look unprofessional in the eyes of the prospect, it could also make them wonder about the business as a whole.

When creating your marketing and information materials, you need to bear in mind that millennials consume media in a different way to previous generations (refer back to Chapter 1 with the stats about the importance of millennials in the buying process). 35% of younger millennials prefer video-based content compared to older millennials (27%), while infographics and webinars seem to resonate least with millennials.

Do you need to spend on anything?
If this is the first time the organisation has gone into such depth and strategic planning, there may be shortfalls in the existing training and tools.

For example:

- A CRM system (Customer Relationship Management)
- A sales funnel
- New marketing materials
- New online platforms
- Training

Get everything lined up and ready before committing to the new strategy; ideally, you want to get it close to right the first time around. Of course, it will change and develop over time, but hit the ground running, have a definitive start date and make sure you measure the outcomes.

Putting the Strategy into Action
After all that hard work planning, it's time to put the Strategy into play.

- Do make sure all the decisions and actions are documented in order to track progress over the year, tweaking if necessary
- Make sure that ALL employees are fully aware of this new Sales Strategy and that they have all bought into it

- Get any new marketing/promo materials ready
- Monitor and track progress
- Keep teams onboard by making sure they are continually updated
- Remember to continually recognise success within your teams
- Thank teams for their work!

Going right back to the basics may seem a bit of a chore, but it will enable you to create a strategy that reflects your aims as a sales leader whilst also respecting what has gone before.

Your Sales Strategy should be flexible enough to account for changing conditions, and you must review it regularly.

Chapter 9

Why a Sales Process is So Important

Let's take a walk through this topic.

What is a Sales Process?

A sales process is a series of steps (processes) designed so a salesperson can guide a prospective buyer from initial interest through to a closed sale…you already know all this, but sometimes a refresher is useful!

There are usually between 5 – 7 identifiable stages.

Why Do You Need One?

Can you imagine trying to do something, anything, in business without having some kind of plan or structure in place by which both expectations and outcomes can be managed?

Picture this, you recruit a new salesperson. They come highly recommended and have a brilliant track record. Yet months down the line, they are failing to reach targets and seem disaffected, so you call them into a meeting to find out what's going on.

The first thing they say is…

"There's no standard procedure, everyone does things their own way. There is no consistency, I don't know what I'm supposed to do, when, or how!"

The only reason they could say this is if there are no systems in place.

There's a bunch of individuals trying their best but without any structure to inform them. It is so important to get your teams and departments working together. A comprehensive Sales Process will help this to happen. Everyone in the organisation will be able to see a cohesive overall sales strategy is in place, and a documented Process will clarify where their particular role sits and what they need to do to make things happen.

Documented and understood processes also mean the sales teams have structure to their selling activities, making it easier to analyse results. For example, if everyone has the same basic guidelines for selling, why do some of the team perform better than others? And, if a Sales Process demonstrably shows results (i.e. increased sales), then your sales team will be fully on board; after all, improving sales will deliver increased remuneration to them.

Sales Processes also form an integral part of Sales Forecasting, as well as being a great way to underline confidence by demonstrating that the strategy is working and that everyone is playing a part in the success.

What About the Customers?

Having a structured process for converting suspects into prospects and then into closed sales will ensure that ALL buyers will experience the same journey.

One of the biggest complaints from customers is that they don't feel valued during the sales process. They are treated as merely a 'sale', not an individual (applicable even if they are acting on behalf of an organisation). Creating a great sales process that documents and tracks a customer's journey through your Sales Funnel (see below) will ensure they receive the right service at the right time and at the right price - hopefully resulting in a sale!

Remember, these days at least 57% of your potential customers will have already made their purchase decision based on online research. And many of them really won't want to interact with you in any way other than online, so you need to be ready to either accept this kind of scenario, or be able to convince them otherwise via your targeted marketing approach and your ongoing Sales Process.

Your Sales Process should improve your NPS (net promoter score) and CSI (customer satisfaction index) considerably so your customers will feel valued and respected, rather than pressured and confused.

What Will You Need to Create Your Sales Process?
A CRM System (Customer Relationship Management)

What is a CRM?

If you have ever used a spreadsheet to track your customer's journey, then you have created your own basic CRM.

You will have recorded:
- The customer name and contact details
- How the lead was gained and when
- Who spoke to them and when
- What their enquiry was (what is it they want to buy)
- Follow up date(s) will have been logged
- Follow up calls logged
- Sale (or not) recorded

A dedicated CRM system can provide a clarity that your spreadsheet would struggle to do (unless you are an absolute Excel wizard!).

Used fully and correctly, your CRM will become a literal data repository for ALL your customer interactions, and it will improve customer relations because your dealings with them will appear seamless even if different team members work with them. It will also improve Customer Lifetime Value (CLV) because your customer base will feel they are known, recognised, and valued. They are therefore more likely to become repeat, even loyal customers.

A sales CRM is often introduced by finance or leadership to "keep the data" if someone leaves. However, the real value comes when sellers see and feel the value of a sales CRM in their day to day activities. A sales leader should therefore have an understanding of and a way to leverage both Control Points and Impact Points.

Sales Pipeline Control Points (leading)
- Awareness: You must have an overview of all your open sales to be able to recognise and guide the effort to the right priorities. Not all customers are the same and if you are treating all your customers the same way, you are failing to target prospects based on their value to your business.
- Assessment: You must know where you are in each deal. You will have lots of opportunities in the sales pipeline, but may feel that you are not able to manage your

prospects and sales activities to effectively complete the sales process.

- Contact Strategy: In B2B sales, there will be several different decision-makers and influencers involved. You need to know where each of them is in the buying cycle and what strategy you have to move them through the cycle to the next stage. The likelihood is the more expensive the product or service you are selling, the more complex the buying team gets.

- Strategy to win: Start with the strategy to win this piece of business, then be clear on the tactics you will use to deliver this specific opportunity and follow with a set of specific actions that move each of these opportunities forward.

- A clear value proposition: Ensure you have a strong value proposition. Without it your deal will have a low probability of success and your customer will not see the value of change. Worse, they might see the value of change but just not with you.

Sales Pipeline Impact Points (lagging)

- Data Accuracy: Ensure the accuracy and the quality of the data in your sales pipeline is in place throughout each opportunity's sales cycle. A sure-fire way to make this happen is by demonstrating to the Account Manager the value in keeping the data accurate by using it in performance reviews and all reporting.

- Win Rate: Knowing your sales pipeline numbers, and what to do to improve them, is what will drive sales. What number of prospects do you need in your pipeline to make your quota? What are your rates through each stage of the sales cycle? Where does attention need to be placed to increase your Win Rate?

- Slippage: Have a realistic date and time stamps to ensure your sales professionals don't keep re-stamping stage commitment dates. This messes up the pipeline numbers and shows unwanted sales behaviour. Using "slippage" data will help you focus your coaching to improve the sales cycle time.

- Stage Velocity: In order to make the right decisions, you need to be in full control of your sales process, know your customer history and how long it takes you to move a lead from prospect to customer. If you don't have this kind of visibility of your sales pipeline you will fail to shorten your sales cycles. If your sales cycles are too long, the problem could be that you have a "leak" somewhere in your sales pipeline.

- Opportunity Advancement: It's all about moving the opportunity forward and seeing that the owner of the opportunity is making progress. Is the customer moving closer to making a buying decision and a buying decision with your company? This is a key measure of success.

These Control Points and Impact Points will lead to more successful sales outcomes and make your Sales Managers masters of the Sales Pipeline Management game

A Sales Funnel
A sales funnel is fundamentally the way you bring your customers closer to your offer and ultimately to a sale. In order for you to track the progress through this sales funnel, you need a way to record all your customer interactions. Hence the importance of a robust CRM system (see above)

At Plan.Grow.Do. we break down the sales process into seven sections:

- Suspect
- Prospect
- Approach
- Negotiate
- Close
- Order
- Pay

Or SPANCOP for short.

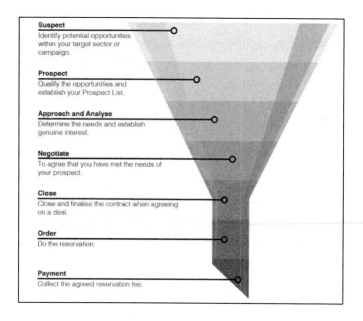

Suspect
Identify potential opportunities within your target sector or campaign.

Prospect
Qualify the opportunities and establish your Prospect List.

Approach and Analyse
Determine the needs and establish genuine interest.

Negotiate
To agree that you have met the needs of your prospect.

Close
Close and finalise the contract when agreeing on a deal.

Order
Do the reservation.

Payment
Collect the agreed reservation fee.

SPANCOP

You should be able to set up your CRM system in such a way that you will be able to label your customers according to their journey through this funnel.

Following the SPANCOP system and recording data accurately within your chosen CRM will allow you to create processes in and around each of the separate headings. This means that if you have different groups or teams working at different levels within your sales team, they will all be fully aware of their part in the overall Sales Process.

Equally, ensuring departments such as marketing and finance are part of the Sales Process and have access to the CRM will smooth the customer journey through the funnel.

Now we'll take a look at each level in a little more detail:

Suspects
Starting at the very top of the funnel – the widest part – this is where you should theoretically have the greatest number of potential customer details. We tag these as 'suspects' – they are the leads, the approaches, the speculative contacts. Get them in your CRM, no matter how speculative, because if you don't record them, how can you hope to track and follow up on them?

Once you have these 'suspects' recorded, you can begin the process of reaching out to them in order to move them further down the funnel. You could use email, phone calls, videos. Your approach should have been set down in your Sales Strategy in conjunction with your marketing team, so your sales teams should be aware of the steps to take.

Prospects

Using the appropriate methods, you should have been able to establish which 'suspects' are legitimate potential customers, and you can move them down the funnel to sit in your 'prospects' section.

These are more qualified leads that you can now begin to work on further to convert to sales.

Approach and Analyse

You now have a 'prospects' list and can begin to reach out to the potential customer in a more personalised way in order to establish that there is a genuine interest. You will need to ascertain the customer's pain points and begin the process of ensuring your offering fits their needs and requirements.

Negotiate

Your list of potential customers (out of the original interest) will have reduced considerably by the time you reach this phase. Arguably this is the most important part of the process as this is where, having already ascertained there is a need for what you are selling, you convince the prospect that this is indeed the case! At the end of this level, you will have either a commitment to purchase, a definite no, or a customer who will remain in the 'negotiate' phase a little longer.

Close

The deal is done – now to the legal side of things, contracts, and agreements. Until everything is agreed and signed, you could still lose the sale.

Don't be tempted to think this stage is a matter of tying up loose ends; keep the dealings efficient and effective.

Order

Well done – you're over the SPANCOP finishing line…well almost! Don't allow your team to become complacent though, they may have done their part in closing the deal but remind them that, to the customer, they are the faces of the organization, their contact point. Make sure that everything is recorded in your CRM. Even little things like knowing the name of a customers' spouse or child could help at some point in the future (remember CLV?).

Payment

Collecting payments should be straightforward, especially if your terms and conditions are stringent. But this needn't be the end of your contact with a customer. Provided you comply with GDPR regs, you should be contacting them on a regular basis, both to see how they are getting on with their purchase and to keep them advised of new products which may also be of interest.

Remember, selling is constantly evolving, as are buyers. You need to make sure that you are able to match their changing requirements by modifying Sales Processes if necessary.

Never rest on past successes – look at businesses such as Kodak, Nokia and IBM…massive multinational companies who failed to recognise changing marketplaces and subsequently collapsed.

Use your Sales Process to communicate with buyers, ask them what it is they want and need. Keep ahead of the game and innovate.

"Selling is about understanding the human brain and how it makes decisions. You can build that skill set through some non-traditional "selling" roles like fundraising, customer retention, or similar roles that require influence and negotiation" (source: LinkedIn poll 2021)

Chapter 10

Lists or Leads?

The previous chapter covered the systems and processes that a successful organisation needs to have in place in order to maximise the sales potential, but when it comes to seeking out potential new customers, how can you be sure you are uncovering the right leads? In other words…

Are You Building Lists, Not Leads?

How many times do you or your partner sit at home and scroll aimlessly through your social feeds, blogs, and websites to have something simply pique your interest? *"Oh look, a guide to help me sleep better"*, *"Top tips on how to get fitter and eat what I like"*, *"The 10 things I need to do before I invest in the stock market"*.

Most of these fancy headlines and free assets have a legitimate use and benefit to the recipient almost *immediately* – it is what they are designed to do. This is the purpose of what becomes known as a *lead magnet*. According to *Investopedia,* a lead magnet is:

…a marketing term for a free item or service that is given away for the purpose of gathering contact details; for example, lead magnets can be trial subscriptions, samples, white papers, e-newsletters, and free consultations.

We [Team Plan.Grow.Do.] think lead magnets are great, don't get us wrong. But there is a real risk that we see these list building exercises and opportunities with a sense of urgency to get something sold with the same immediacy in which the prospect so nonchalantly downloaded the content in the first place.

It's never been easier to build lists. It's how Facebook and the other social media giants make their fortune; by selling your data!

The problem we are seeing more and more is that this may well be creating unrealistic and meaningless KPI's and expectations on those in the sales function. This can create disquiet across the departments, even though neither are in the wrong and both may actually be hitting a realistic target, but our attention is focused elsewhere, and we don't see the real results.

The problem may be in what we are measuring in the first place.

We see businesses driving behaviours to hit targets, and there is a list of hundreds of names and numbers, yet the conversion is nil or limited. Why is this? Perhaps there is more focus on the *output* rather than the *outcome*, meaning the list volume is measurable output and, if we assume this to be a qualified list of suitable leads in which to measure our sales performance, we are missing out on the opportunity to measure, manage and adjust our sales efforts in a more meaningful – outcome focused – way.

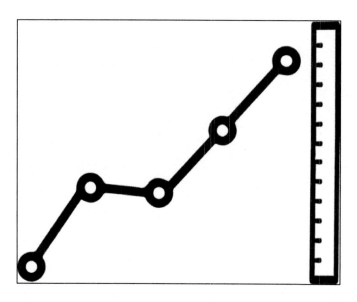

How Much Do Lists & Leads Cost?

According to Databox, the average cost per lead sits about $25 (£20). But our concern is that Facebook has changed the language to assume that anyone in a list is a lead, and therefore are treated as a *hot one* and should be followed up as if they are ready to buy. But we must ask ourselves, *are all leads really the same?* To help us understand this, let's take a look at demystifying some jargon that we might be tangled in!

MQL and SQL

What is an MQL – a Marketing Qualified Lead?

According to Evenbound, an MQL (Marketing Qualified Lead) is a reasonably qualified lead who has downloaded a content offer or interacted with your marketing team but who hasn't yet entered into your sales funnel.

What is an SQL – a Sales Qualified Lead?

So we have a stack of MQL's – but what's next? What, by definition, is an SQL?

An SQL (Sales Qualified Lead) is a lead your sales team has qualified as a potential customer. SQLs are in your sales funnel, and your team is actively working to move them closer to a deal.

Can You See the Gap?

By building lists of prospects whom we assume are already in a buying mood, we are putting a lot of pressure on sales teams to hit numbers based on a list of people who, in reality, have signaled *zero* interest in actually *buying* what we want to sell them.

So Why the Disparity in Lists and Sales Success?

In a very interesting piece of research we stumbled across on LinkedIn, it was suggested that a whopping 98% of marketing lists never turn in to customers. So only 2% of those people are in any sort of position or mindset to buy something from you.

We *know* deep down that just because we downloaded an interesting report, an effective how-to or a whitepaper relating to our industry, it doesn't mean *we* are ready to buy, yet when we hop over into our sellers' shoes, we *expect* our latest list addition to be ready to jump at the opportunity to buy our stuff!

So What Are You Measuring Your Success in Sales On?

Create Prospects, Not Leads.
In the absence of any qualification from your lists or your marketing activity, or any definition in the *urgency* in which this potential prospect emerges in your sales universe, you run the risk of trying to *sell your stuff* to people who simply don't know who you are.

A sales team needs to contribute to better marketing conversations to help *create Prospects not leads.*

How can you Measure Sales Outcomes Based on Marketing Output?
If you measure your sales team on marketing output and expect them to be effectively closing on their targets, you may risk affecting their confidence. By applying better measurement to your structures and processes, you can see with much more relevance the results and numbers that are more meaningful to the whole team.

Not All Leads Are the Same
To re-iterate – we think lists are good, very good! A solid and growing list of the best kind of suspects in your ecosystem and sales universe can only be a good thing. But to assume these leads are in the same buying phase or buying moment as someone who sees the '*need help fast*' emergency number on your website is misguided.

A casual social scroller downloading some sector insights is not the same as a person seeking out a website, search result or phone number. They are each coming to you with a different purpose; the former you are interrupting their space, the latter you are answering a pre-defined problem they have. Two very distinct differences that should help us understand that not all leads are of the same quality, immediacy, or opportunity for success.

It's Not Sales or Marketing Anymore, It's Sales *and* Marketing

It is important to look beyond 'job snobbery' or the assumption your role is above, below or beyond your remit. *Every* role in your organisation should have a customer-centric approach to its application.

If you allow internal politics and operational tendencies to prevent you from developing an effective and aligned approach, you run the real risk of not being as effective in your outcomes as you would like.

And What Is Customer-Centricity?

According to Gartner, customer-centricity is *"...the ability of people in an organisation to understand customers' situations, perceptions, and expectations. Customer centricity demands that the customer is the focal point of all decisions related to delivering products, services and experiences to create customer satisfaction, loyalty and advocacy."*

If your operational behaviour is focused solely on the output of the sales team and is in fact measuring the wrong thing, how can you genuinely be putting the customer at the heart of your business? If we can take a step back and consider how our sales team impact on the outcomes we desire, not the outputs of misaligned KPI's, we think you can find better customer focused activity across the business.

So what can you do to ensure you are building better leads, not just creating lists?

- Lead scoring. Not all leads are the same quality, yet if you treat the measurable output as simply one master list of data and treat them as hot leads, you could find yourself frustrated
- Listen to feedback from the customer. Are you capturing and listening to feedback about the real customer experience?
- Create better customer personas. We find the benefits of building out customer personas to include better communications, better relationships, more efficient sales teams, and better marketing. But what benefits can *you* find in really creating customer personas?
- Build a content plan across the sales process, not just at the top. How can your sales team be more active in the early stages of the buying journey, and what would that

best customer persona expect to engage with at this moment in their buying journey?

- Be aware that just because someone is aware of you, it doesn't mean they are ready to buy
- Engage sales professionals at the top of the process to work *with* marketing. Your sales team most likely connect with the emotions of your best customers, but how is this fed back to support the marketing effort to build new MQL's for the team to filter out the SQL's?
- Collaborate. We must remove the silo culture in business and by collaborating we will create, over time, a customer centric and future proofed joined up approach to buying and selling

Chapter 11

Sales Training

We've covered in some detail the underlying framework an organisation needs to have in place in order to maximise the sales potential and actually stay in business, but what part could sales training play in the process?

Sales training…what is it good for?

Well, unless you have all the other basics in place as covered earlier, the answer is…

Absolutely nothing!

As the sales leader in your organisation, you can put your teams through any number of sales training courses, and there are thousands of them (just run a Google search and see for yourself), but it's a bit like learning online how to snow ski whilst living in Equatorial New Guinea...the knowledge may be there, but it can't be put into action or practice as the conditions are wrong!

OK, that's maybe a bit of a tortured analogy, but hopefully you get the point!

Now we aren't saying that sales training can't be useful, it's actually what Plan.Grow.Do. is all about after all, but you need to examine:

- Why your team need training
- What you hope to get out of it (ROI)
- How you will measure the success (outcomes)
- How any training sits within your overall sales strategy

Let's have a look in more detail at these bullet points.

Why Does Your Team Need Training?

- Is it because your sales figures have dropped/are dropping?
- Do you have a new product?
- Are you targeting a new market sector?
- Do you have a lot of new starters?

Many businesses will offer training to their staff 'because it's the right thing to do'. And indeed, in terms of staff development and retention, training *is* often the right thing to offer within part of an overall Personal Development Plan (PDP).

The problem is that a 2 day 'improve your selling technique' course is not going to be much good if the course content takes no account of the specific needs of your people *or* the organisation as a whole. Think back to the skiing analogy above!

Similarly, sending people off on expensive courses without ensuring they will be able to put what they have learned into practice once they get back is counterproductive. It is also demoralising for them and for the organisation as a whole.

If you put training in place for your people, there also needs to be some kind of tracking and follow up process in order to ensure that learning is retained. There are studies that indicate people will lose 80%-90% of whatever was learned during training within one month! What a waste of their time and your money. You needn't necessarily set tests for people, but you should have a framework in place to allow learnings to be validated; it could simply be a case of asking your salespeople to reference an aspect of training they found useful/helped them close a sale.

What Do You Hope to Get Out of It?
Before investing thousands on sending your staff on courses (or on bringing the courses on-site), stop and work out just what the goal is.

What outcomes are you looking to achieve, and what sort of ROI (return on investment) do you expect. ROI need not necessarily be financial by the way.

Do you expect sales figures to increase as a result? If so, by how much and in what timescale?

Remember, '*On average, only 29% of sales reps hit performance milestones in their first year. – Aberdeen, 2013*'. If you are sending your new sales employees on training, will it actually improve on that figure? If it turns out it doesn't, is it the right training?

Conversely, if you are looking for a 'softer' approach to ROI, will training add to company culture, staff retention and staff satisfaction levels?

Offering training for training's sake, in other words, a tick box exercise, won't benefit the bottom line or staff's wellbeing and success rates.

How Are You Going to Measure the Outcomes of Training?
Remember the quote above that says people will forget 80 to 90% of everything they learn on a course if you don't follow up with them? How are you going to do that? It's pretty pointless sending people for training if you don't then ensure they retain and use the knowledge.

So, will you arrange for tests to check on them, and what level will you accept as 'good' or a 'pass'?

Will you check sales figures before and after training to see if there is a difference, and what will you accept as being a sufficient increase to justify the training?

If taking the softer PDP approach to ROI, when will you check in with your teams? Just after training? One week later? Six months later?

How Does Training Fit Within Your Overall Sales Strategy?

Training isn't cheap, and if you are going to invest in upskilling your team, you need to ensure that the courses they take are fit for YOUR purpose. Any training must not only be relevant and something your teams need, it must also sit within the organisation's culture.

If you have the capability, it may be advisable to spend your training budget on developing an in-house training provision in order that the training is specific, measurable, achievable, relevant and timely for your unique requirements. Yes, this is a reference to using SMART (goals) as a way of checking that the training you provide your teams is actually what they *and* the organisation need.

This doesn't mean that you shouldn't purchase 'off the shelf packages', simply that bespoke training content will be far more effective and, with an in-house setup, it should be easier to provide the 'follow up' mentioned earlier. And you are a Sales Leader - doesn't it make more sense to have a hand in developing the most appropriate training for your people?

"I've seen good leaders come from other parts of the company, Supply, HR, but they are more Admin than Sales Driver, High Powered sales leaders know how to sell the product, but more important than being the best salesperson, they should be the best Trainer, so a great leader doesn't have to be the BEST salesperson, but needs the knowledge and the ability to train and mentor" CEO energy sector (source: LinkedIn poll 2021)

How Can Training Be Implemented in The Organisation?
There is a lot of good and valuable training out there, but stop and think how training can be made a part of the organisation's culture rather than be seen as a nice bolt-on for new starters.

Continuous professional development (CDP) is as vital for a salesperson as for any other professional, and it should be treated with the respect it deserves.

Sending staff off on training days every now and again with no system for post-training reinforcement and no idea if the courses themselves are fit for purpose is a waste of resources.

As a leader in the sales industry, you may already be involved in training your teams - have a look at what you're doing and see if you may benefit from some CPD and training yourself. In this post-pandemic world we now live in, things are changing every day, and it's up to you to ensure that your skills are kept up to date.

How Are Sales Training Course Delivered?
As you would expect, just as there are lots of different courses, there are different ways of delivering them.

These include:

- Online one to one or group delivery via Zoom/Skype etc
- Workshops – face to face OR online
- Home study via email/video/workbooks
- Traditional classroom
- Facebook groups

Ultimately though, however the training is delivered if you don't take in to account the advice in this chapter, you could be literally spending money for nothing.

Epilogue

We hope this journey through sales leadership has left you with thoughts around what you want your business to be known for.

What do you want people to say about your company's culture when you aren't in the room and what does good look like for your business in the short term and longer-term views?

While you may assume that any culture derived in business is only seen from and towards sales management to the sales executive, please do consider the role of all departments in the business.

How the leadership create the space for management to thrive is woven into the cultural development of the business.

Your sales culture must contribute to business outcomes of course and you can expect substantial benefits around staff churn, staff performance and demand. A healthy competition that is fostered in the right environment can expect to outperform competition.

Your staff will be happier, we know this because research carried out by Columbia University tells us that you typically see a 13.9% staff turnover vs 48.4% turnover in a more outdated business, with 70% of sales execs leaving their role because of a breakdown in communication with their direct line manager.

A last question for you. What do Google, Adobe, Samsung, Microsoft and HubSpot all have in common?

You've probably worked this out by now. You've got it, they have incredibly sound organisational cultures. We know this because in a 2021 these brands ranked top when it came to corporate culture.

What else do they have in common? Well, they all operate in incredibly competitive fields and excel in in terms of sales and revenue.

We now believe you're with us when we say, good leadership breeds a robust culture which breeds loyalty and performance which breeds long lasting sales success.

You now know how you can impact positively on the leadership and business culture within your organisation to create a legacy.

Now go make it happen!

References

Foreword: 'Funnel Vision – Selling Made EASY' is available from Amazon www.amzn.to/31MrHA9

Page 4:
https://www.juanvilar.com/the-code-of-hammurabi-and-the-regulation-of-the-olive-oil-trade/
https://pharmaceutical-journal.com/article/opinion/the-history-of-snake-oil
https://history-computer.com/john-patterson-complete-biography/

Page 5:
https://www.retailtimes.co.uk/76-of-uk-consumers-research-or-get-inspiration-online-before-they-make-a-purchase-um-reports/

Page 7:
https://www.adaptworldwide.com/insights/2021/b2b-marketing-for-gen-z-millennial-buyers
https://www.aflac.com/about-aflac/corporate-citizenship/corporate-social-responsibility-report/default.aspx

Page 10:
https://uniquity.co/insights/70-sales-decision-really-made-face-face-meeting/

Page 11:
https://www.bls.gov/news.release/pdf/tenure.pdf

https://www.inc.com/peter-economy/the-millennial-workplace-of-future-is-almost-here-these-3-things-are-about-to-change-big-time.html
https://www.conecomm.com/research-blog/2016-millennial-employee-engagement-study

Page 15:
https://bizbible.org/
https://ziftsolutions.com/blog/sales-marketing-alignment-best-practices/#:~:text=67%25%20higher%20probability%20that%20marketing,108%25%20better%20lead%20acceptance
https://www.forrester.com/bold (Sirius acquired by Forrester)

Page 18:
https://www.scci.org.uk/Data/News_Downloads/SYSkills report.pdf?date=28/04/2021%2006:55:21

Page 27:
https://hbr.org/2015/09/the-7-attributes-of-the-most-effective-sales-leaders
https://www.gwi.com/

Page 37:
https://databox.com/lower-cost-per-lead-from-facebook-ads
https://evenbound.com/

Page 38:
https://www.gartner.com/en/marketing/glossary/customer-centricity

Page 40:

https://learningsolutionsmag.com/articles/1379/brain-science-the-forgetting-curvethe-dirty-secret-of-corporate-training

https://www.anaplan.com/wp-content/uploads/2013/09/Aberdeen-Group-Motivate-Incent-Compensate-Enable.pdf

Services

Plan.Grow.Do. are a sales training organisation helping business owners, sales teams and business leaders find the confidence, process and structure to succeed in sales.

Plan.Grow.Do. help traditional sales teams sell more. They help companies identify their evolving buyers' buying journey and address changes in the sales world.

They do this through a variety of training solutions that support the sales function at all levels of the business.

For more about the services available from Plan.Grow.Do. and to see how they've helped people just like you, please visit:
www.plangrowdo.com

Printed in Great Britain
by Amazon